I Am Str

MW00983296

I Am Str

Copyright © April 10, 2017
by Jermika R. Williams

Unless otherwise indicated scripture taken from the King James Version®.
Copyright © 182 by Thomas Nelson. Used by permission. All rights reserved.

ISBN-13: 978-1545126110

ISBN-10: 1545126119

☐ ***I am Strong:***
- o Great in intellectual and physical power
- o Effective and efficient
- o Not easily disturbed

☐ ***I am Bold:***
- o Fearless before danger
- o A Fearless and daring spirit
- o Prominently standing out

☐ ***I am Beautiful:***
- o Natural beauty
- o Pleasing to the mind and spirit
- o Graceful and brilliant

☐ ***I am Free:***
- o Rights of a citizen (Kingdom citizen)
- o Relieved from lacking anything
- o Not restricted by qualifications

"I cannot heal the things you accept"...

thus saith the Lord 05/29/16

TABLE OF CONTENTS

Forward

I am now 35 years old and walking in my God given purpose and call on my life. For many years I asked God, "What is my purpose?" I asked him for clarity on the things I have been through. You see, I went on a journey from not knowing Him at all, to becoming an acquaintance and then into full intimacy. I met a savior named Jesus Christ and He told me all about who I was to Him. He explained many things about me that I, in turn will share with you. This book seemed to be birthed rapidly. It was born in less than sixty days. However, it was in me for years. God used the man I was sleeping with over 5 years ago to tell me there was a book in me. Did I shock you by admitting that? If so, you may be shocked as you read the rest of this journey. It took me so long to put pen to paper because I knew it would hurt. I knew what would flow out of me would be painful, yet liberating. I knew it would be like the pains of childbirth, like the agony of delivery followed by immense joy once the baby is born. So when God told me you have until April 1st to get it done, I was more than ready. It's funny how God works sometimes. He knows what He told me years ago, yet He waited for me. It's funny how He used my greatest skill of working best under pressure to birth my story of deliverance. You see, I thought I was delivered. In my mind, I am functioning and moving as a minister and servant to a ministry of deliverance. Of course I am delivered. I had to rethink that when He required such a quick turnaround for my story. I asked God for some things along the way and He was ready to give them to me but there were deep roots that could not follow me into this promise land. When you run into your purpose, you will come to find out that your promise is right around the corner from it. God put a burden on my heart for the women who are survivors of sex trafficking. Literally, He showed me women coming home from being used and abused and they needed restoration. I always thought, why me? I have never been a survivor of sex trafficking. Well in the process of writing this book I found out exactly why me. The Lord gave me a mantra this year that I heard one day driving my car. He said to me, "I am Strong, Bold, Beautiful and Free." He required me to say it multiple times. I repeated it to myself but didn't fully believe it. You see, there was a little girl trapped inside of me. She grew up wondering if she was bold. She felt strong at times, but could she say she was strong? Other's told her she was beautiful but the rejection said she wasn't. But today I can say that I am the woman of God that my Savior has shaped and formed to use for His glory. And I am Strong, Bold, Beautiful and finally...... Free.

Who Am I? Chapter 1

There is nothing like walking through life wondering if you are the real you. As we grow from day to day and year to year, have we really evolved into who we were predestined to be? Did I wake up one morning and decide this is the woman I will be? As I look back over the 35 years of my life I realize that I had a destiny. He predestined me. God did…… before I even knew him He knew me. He decided beforehand that He would use me. He decided that every piece of my life He would use for His glory one day. If I could go back in time for a moment…. I remember settling in, in elementary school in Springfield, Massachusetts. I had moved around so much. It seemed like every year, I was in a new school. I lived with my mom throughout the week and went for weekends most times with my dad. It was just my mom and I and usually a boyfriend she dated. I actually think we moved to Massachusetts with my mom's boyfriend but that is somewhat of a blur. It was a nice place. It was way better than the place we lived before. We usually had our own place but there were times we stayed at other peoples' homes. As long as it didn't have mice and roaches like the other place, it was cool. I remember one time we had an apartment where a robber got in. My mom was so angry. They took some of my toys and our radio system. I remember her yelling outside to the neighbors that she knows they saw something and to return her stuff, especially her kid's stuff. We didn't stay there very long. I don't remember how and when we transitioned to Massachusetts, but it was a brand new place and atmosphere for us. No matter who was there with us, all I ever saw was my mom and I.

It seemed like every year, I was in a new school For some reason I thought, ok maybe this will be it. We will settle down here and I will meet and keep some new friends. I didn't mind playing by myself but I was open to actually having friends. The school was tough because I noticed there weren't a lot of kids there that looked like me. There was one kid who taunted me every day as we waited in line for the school bus. He called me names I had never heard of. I told my mom about those names and to say the least, she was up at that school. My mom was so amazing to me. She was always there! She would cook for me as I sat at our brown glass table in the kitchen. I remember the bucket chairs that use to swivel back and forth. She was so pretty too. She reminded me of the lady on the show A Different World, I think her name was Whitley. As I look back and reminisce on my life as a child I can't help but to see all the times God showed me He set me apart. Like the time I wrote the President of the United States. I was determined to know why there were only five books in the library on black history. Now that I think back, I really didn't want the books but it was the principal of the matter. I asked anyone who would listen why don't we have more books and no one could give me an answer. All I ever wanted was an answer. My mom told me to do something about it. So I went to school and asked my teacher what could I do about it and she told me to write the President. Who knows if she was being sarcastic but from that moment I was on a mission. I wrote the letter and handed it into my teacher and she said she would mail it. Assignment complete! Still to this day my mind focuses on, assignment complete!

As a young girl I was charged to ask the hard questions and not settle for bogus answers. This was over 25 years ago and I can remember this event like it was yesterday. My short term memory is horrible but my long-term is surely intact! A few months later after black history month had come and gone, a call came into my teacher's classroom. She said in front of the whole class, "Jermika you have a letter from the President in the office." I was the outcast, the last one picked, and the peculiar one but in that moment, I was the center of attention. I was so proud to walk down that hall. All the teachers and students were looking at me as I walked down the hallway Well, I think they were. Either way that's how it felt! They gave me a letter with a gold seal on it with my name. I was so proud that day. My mom was so proud of me for standing up for something I believed in. Today I can truly say He predestined me. It's interesting how one of the most momentous occasions in my life can also be connected with a troublesome event. Sometimes we only like to discuss the glory of a story, but there were times when your election of being predestined came with a test.

I remember walking to the bus stop, I had to be about 10 or 11 years old. My mom went to work in the mornings so I walked to the bus stop across the street. No one was out there that morning, just me. A car pulled up and opened the door and told me to get in. I didn't know this man and he scared me. I dropped my book bag and took off. I remember running to my apartment building and hiding in the hallway. I was terrified. What does that man want with me? I recall going to a neighbor for help and she called my mom. I don't remember what came of that, but I know the story could have gone another way. Unbeknownst to me, God was with me. I don't know how I knew to react the way I did, but God saved me and He kept me.

As a young girl I always felt somewhat different. I would even see and hear things that I couldn't express to others. I now know it was a gift from God. I just didn't seem to fit in. All I ever wanted to do was fit in. I wanted normalcy. I found out that the family and world I only ever knew was not the same world other's lived in. I found out that everyone didn't move around a lot. I came to find out that not everyone lived with their mom and went to their dads on the weekend. I didn't see many marriages in my family where there was not a blended family of some sort. The women were always the strong ones leading the pack. Is that the order of marriage? Speaking of strong woman, I had my grandmother in my life. My mom's mother was always a woman of interest to me. She seemed to have everything. She lived in a big house in Atlanta and drove fancy cars. She always seemed so put together. One day in elementary school, I remember going down to Atlanta and staying there. I loved visiting grandma but this time it wasn't a visit, I was staying. Where was my mom? Why was I living here with grandma? These were the questions that swirled in my head. I don't recall ever asking them but they were there. I was away from my mother and my father and I didn't know why? Was it me? Did I do something wrong? I heard my mom was in rehab or something but I didn't really understand what for. I remember seeing my mom do things I knew weren't right, but she was perfect to me... so whatever! Now, here I am, being raised on raisin bran and rye bread by two older people. Life became routine in Atlanta but it was never home.

Where was my father? Why am I miles away and he lived in the same state? I used to go over his house every other weekend faithfully. He was a good father and always there, but this time, he was not. I shrugged it off. Maybe I couldn't live at his house with his family.

He had a wife and they had two sons. I didn't always like going over there. It wasn't because they didn't treat me well, I just never knew what to do. They sat at the table and ate, we didn't do that at home. Things were just so different from one house to the other. I always felt like I was walking on pins and needles. I remember lying a lot. I knew lying was wrong but I would lie to make our life at my mom's house seem just as elaborate as theirs. All these thoughts are going through my mind but never did I express them. My dad would call me and check up on me in Atlanta, so I knew that he knew where I was. There were times I wanted to ask him why haven't you come to get me? I remember one time my dad and family came down to visit to go to Disney World. It was awesome! I felt a sense of normalcy again. It was still awkward at times, but at least it was familiar. I remember when they were leaving, I wondered if my dad would miss me. I wondered if it was hard to leave me there.

I don't remember how long I stayed, it couldn't have been for the past few months. But one day I got a phone call. It was my mom. She told me she wanted me to come home. She said she got a new place and was dating a new guy. I remember telling her "I feel like you chose him over me. Why am I living with grandma and grandpa?" I can remember my mom crying and I felt bad. I would never want to hurt my mom. You see, my mom could do no wrong in my eyes.

She was always there with me. It was always me and her no matter who was in the picture. No matter what I witnessed, the good or bad, I had her back. So she told me she had to get her life together to be better for me and that she was in a better place. She sent for me to come home and so I went back to Connecticut. It was time for middle school. I was in a new town and entering a new stage of life, but I was back with my mom. We lived in an apartment where I had my own room. I always had my own room when we had an apartment so it was to be expected. We had a dog too. I don't recall ever having a dog before this one. As time went on, my mom told me she was going to get married. I was happy for her. She deserved to be married. She had never been married outside of my father so I was happy for her. The guy was cool too. I remember we had a nice car also, it was a purple Cadillac with leather seats. Life was good. I was meeting new friends and settling in very well.

In school I began to be interested in boys and my mom used to tell me it was too soon. I used to think what does she know, I already knew about sex and so much more. I held a secret that I now know as a woman was wrong. Being interested in sex was nothing new to me. I had been touched intimately by a loved one for years. I never said anything because I trusted him and figured he knew what was right. I was never penetrated but a seed of promiscuity was planted. My body was awakened to desire arousal and I knew what it felt like. It was only a matter of time before I explored a little deeper. As a woman, I realize that these inappropriate encounters were a part of the pattern of promiscuity I faced as a young adult. I'll talk more about that as we go on but I thank God for healing. To be honest with you, I am experiencing healing now as I type these words from my heart to you. God told me it's time to release the little girl trapped inside of me. I am literally walking through my life's journey and dropping off the baggage at each rest stop. I am becoming who I really am.

So back to middle school, I hadn't done anything sexual yet but I was ready. Needless to say, God spared me from myself. I got through middle school fairly ok. My hormones were suppressed with staying busy and it seemed like God kept me from opportunities of temptation. Again, life was good. I started going back over my dad's on the weekends just like before but just not as frequent. I was getting older and wanted to spend time with my friends and cousins. We stayed in Vernon, Connecticut most of middle school I believe. It may have been the longest we stayed anywhere. My mom was doing well and I was doing well. Along the way my mom decided to get a divorce. He was a nice guy, but truth be told, the divorce didn't bother me. Even in my early teens, I still saw it as just mom and I. We were a team. No matter what distance or circumstances separated us for a season, when we were together, it was right. I was coming to know what love meant from one person to another. Meeting boys and the experiences of my life thus far had me wondering about my thoughts and feelings. I now know that I always felt my parents loved me, but the circumstances behind my life would make me wonder. I don't recall my dad really saying I love you to me, but he always provided and was there when I needed him. On the other hand, my mom told me she loved me all the time but my experience going to Atlanta caused me to feel otherwise. As a woman, I now realize they loved me the best way they knew how.

I am now a mother and realize how our own hang-ups, let-downs and failures affect how our children feel and think, but doesn't always represent truth. Do parents love their children when they fall into drugs? Yes. Do parents love their children when divorce happens? Yes. There comes a point in the life of that child when they become aware of the power of choice. Do they choose to forgive? Do they listen to their hearts? Some will listen, others will close up and resist while claiming to know it all.

The Know It All Complex: Chapter 2

All throughout my high school years I was told I will go to college and the importance of good grades to get accepted. The years flew by like days and before I knew it, it was time to start preparing for my future. I was so self-sufficient and moved so quietly that my parents were not truly involved in my process of making decisions. I went on college tours alone, matter of fact I don't recall even telling them about the tours. I can't blame them for my level of disconnect, it had become a part of who I was. I knew it all and didn't need their help. They didn't offer it and I didn't need it. That was my mind set. I had a job since the moment I turned 16. I applied for jobs on my own and got them on my own. My father would assist me when I asked but I rarely asked. I had two boyfriends in high school that gave me what I thought love was, so I really didn't look outside of them and myself to affirm me.

It's now junior year and I am in a new high school. You see, I had spent freshman and sophomore year living with my aunt and her family in Manchester, CT and one day found out my aunt and uncle were getting a divorce and I needed to go live with my father. I had never lived with him before, but I was so used to being uprooted it didn't matter at this point. I moved in with my aunt and her family whom I loved. I don't recall why I was no longer living with my mom again but at least I was going to be with my cousins. They were like sisters and brothers to me. I shared a room with my favorite cousin, so things were good. I no longer worried about why or where my mom was or even my father's home for that matter. He had some struggles at home as well and now I find out it's time to go. I just figured, let me get myself together and create the life I want to live and that is exactly what I did.

It was almost the perfect time if any, my best friend had just moved to Windsor, CT now I could be with her. So I called my dad and let him know what was going on and he opened his home with open arms. I remember wondering why it was so easy this time but wasn't before when I moved to Georgia. Now, I am almost an adult and I will create a stable life for myself. Life in Windsor was good. I learned so much about being a lady from the influences at my school. My step-mother also tried very hard to make me feel comfortable, although at times I felt like there was a competition for my father's love. Truth is, I really didn't know them. Over the years I went to my dad's house less frequently due to me wanting to be with my friends and cousins. Living with them was an entirely different story. They sat at the kitchen table to eat, cleaned together and we even had breakfast together with daily affirmations. I must admit today, the breakfast and daily affirmations is a memory that I embrace. As a teenager it was a bit ridiculous to me but I continue this tradition with my daughter. I enjoy making something for her to start her day and speaking words of encouragement into her. But back then it was a waste of time. I got decent grades but no one really checked. I was pretty responsible and did what I was supposed to do. I loved working and making my own money. I had a boyfriend who was kind to me when we were together but unfortunately was kind to every other girl when we weren't. When prom time came, no one took me to shop for a dress, and no one asked me what I needed. I did it all from my hair to the dress. My dad provided me with a rental car though. I paid him for it, but he came through for me. I remember asking if my mom could come to see me go to prom but the answer was no. It hurt me so bad that I could not just do what normal families do. None of my friends had this issue. As usual, I have to coordinate and manage both sides of my family in a life I never created. They created me, yet I am always having to adjust to the decisions and factors of their lives. The wall that prohibited my reception and outflow of love definitely resurrected and became higher in my teenage years. I had so many unanswered questions about my life that it was easier to just build the wall then to deal with the emotions.

Junior year in high school, when everyone was making college preparations and selections I had no idea what

I was about to do. My best friend and I said we are going to Clark Atlanta. We had no idea how or why but we were going. The reality set in that there are no savings for college, I am a B-C student so the scholarships are not going to pour in. I heard the Army was recruiting in the cafeteria. I went to the meeting and that same day I took the application home and told my parents I wanted to sign up. I was 17 years old and convinced this is my only way to have independence and get to college. So my parents talked with me and signed for permission for me to enlist in the United States Army. My destiny was going to start off being the possession of the government. I signed up and began going to monthly drills and preparing for when I graduated. I got to senior year and graduated with subpar grades and was ready to start my new journey. I didn't even think about it. I was not afraid, nervous or even having expectations. I was numb. I felt it was what I needed to do not even what I wanted to do. I never really did what I wanted to do, I tended to do what I needed to do most times. I was dating a boy from high school when I left but of course it was about to be over; he is going to college and I was going to the army. I was in a committed relationship with this young man and was sexually active. I had become sexually active at 14 years old but after losing my virginity, I waited a few years before being sexually active again. I thought I was in love with him and so we would have unprotected sex and not worry about the consequences. The worst thing that could happen is that I would get pregnant and then we would just be loving parents. It was a complete illusion. None the less I went to the army without any children and worry free. They broke me down when I got there. I didn't realize how undisciplined I was. I had been living by the seat of my pants for all this time and the structure was necessary. I knew absolutely no one except one girl that I went to school with that I never spoke to. These people didn't know me. I felt like I could create whatever world I wanted to. So that is just what I did. I left my world of Jermika and became Private Williams. I met so many new people and was making my own money with no bills. I hated the army but I loved the freedom. I would write home to my boyfriend and he would write me back but I knew he was dating other girls while he was in college. I met another soldier that I swore I was in love with. How can you be in love with someone you have only known for six weeks and can only talk by passing notes and during chow? But I was in love. We had planned to get married when we graduated from AIT school after basic. Yes it was planned and was going to happen. We got a weekend pass one weekend and went to the hotel to consummate our love. I barely knew anything about this man but we were in love and now having sex. It was unprotected sex at that. Talk about living on the razors edge. I went home for Christmas break from basic training and didn't feel good. I felt like something was wrong with my female parts and I went to the doctor. I found out I had a sexually transmitted disease. From the one I loved and was to marry! I was devastated. Thank God it was a disease curable by medication. I knew better than this, I had been introduced to God at 14 but I didn't need Him in my teenage years because I was in control but this time I thanked Him. I thanked Him for not allowing me to have a disease that would kill me and that I had another chance to get it right. I informed my new love that it was over and that I was moving on before it even began. I never looked back. Was that love? How can you move on so quickly when it is love? I got back focused on what I was supposed to be doing and that is preparing for my future. I went back to basic training and finished the most challenging assignment of my life. I graduated from boot camp and everyone's family was there to see them accomplish one of the greatest challenges in a soldier's life, but mine. I smiled and received my diploma of completion and encouraged myself. I was used to standing alone but I declared my children will never stand alone. Little did I know, that very declaration was about to quickly be challenged in my life. In the most liberating time of my life, I am about to find myself in the greatest level of bondage and captivity. I graduated and was going home for a week before heading to AIT training. The hard part was done and now I needed to be trained on the job I was to complete.

Can I take a vulnerable moment with you as the reader? As I am writing this down for the world to see I can't help but pause because many of the accounts I am testifying to have never been released from my mouth. This liberation is not only necessary, but is freeing me from the very depths of my life's painful accounts. Now... let me continue. I came home and fell into what was familiar. I was in the best shape of my life, my mind has been transformed into a soldier and all I desired was something familiar. Over the last six weeks I barely recognized myself and just wanted something that looked remotely like my life. I linked up with my old boyfriend who was also home from college for winter break. You would think I would have learned my lesson from the last mishap with Mr. Right, but I hooked up with my ex-boyfriend and again had unprotected sex. It was only right. We had been together for a long time, for like a year. It may have been one of the longest relationships I had ever had. I am being facetious as I say this (lol). So we had a week long rendezvous. We both knew nothing new was going to come of this because I was in the service and he was away at college. So I went back to my life of a soldier and continued on with building my life. About 4 weeks after being back at training. I felt very sick. I went to the infirmary thinking I come down with a bug. I had a bug alright, that bug was called an embryo. I was pregnant. I was pregnant, away from home, single and again alone. What do I do from here? I called back home to tell my baby's father and his question was is it mine? Of course it's yours...I think. Either way I was pregnant and I believed it to be his. I didn't believe I was further along than us being together, but life got real, real quick. What could happen, actually happened! I am screwed. I went to church with the rest of the platoon and cried my eyes out. I hadn't talked to God in a few years and I had messed up big time. My career in the army was now jeopardized and now I am 19 about to have a baby. I called back home and told my mother and father. My mother was devastated and told me the choice would be up to me whether I would have the baby or not. My father told me you cannot bring a baby to my house. So now I am stuck. I am alone facing the biggest decision of my life and I am facing abortion or being homeless. I am only 19 years old, but I can do this. I have been in worse conditions than this and made it. I can do this. I just knew I wanted to go home. The Army told me I can be honorably discharged for family life choice. What about the years I have already served, what about college? What about my life? I had to make a decision. I decided I would make my decision whether to keep my baby at home amongst my family. I signed the dotted line to be released from the army and to go home. I flew home feeling hopeless and unaccomplished. The very thing I started off on my own has failed. The spirit of unworthiness crept into my life at that very instant. Doubt and shame followed right behind it. What would people say? What would I tell people? This secret followed me until this day. But thank you God for your liberty. For whom the Son sets free is free indeed. Your secrets can be the very thing that is holding you captive even after the rest of the world has forgotten. I decided to end my pregnancy. I made the decision alone, recuperated alone and walked in the shame alone. The know it all, knew absolutely nothing. It seemed the only thing I knew was failure and pain. I lied my way through many of the questions and whispers of those around me. I was walking around with a heart of stone. I still smiled, I still pressed, but I was dying. All I ever wanted was to be loved, do well and experience what I saw others experiencing. However, God had a plan for my life. He told me "all things work together for the good of them that love God and are called according to His purpose." So He used all my mistakes and my circumstances toward who He called me to be.

I started going back to church here and there and enrolled myself in community college. I again walked into the campus alone, filled out the paperwork and tried to press the restart on what I had terribly messed up. It is amazing how I started school free of charge and more focused than I had ever been. I felt like I had something to prove to my family and to myself. The University of Connecticut was now in my view and I was going to get there if it killed me. I was an A student and did everything I was advised to do to transfer to University of CT. I did two years of community college and applied to UCONN and was accepted. I worked hard. I had two jobs and went to school at night. I worked tirelessly to meet my goals of graduating from college. I was being restored. I got my own apartment, worked, went to school and had a car I paid for in cash. I felt like my life had done a 360. I even started to go back to church more regularly and listening to the word of God. I had yet to truly apply it to my life but I was surely listening. I always felt what I heard was for "them" and not applicable to me, but oh how wrong I was. You see, His riches in glory belonged to me too. His love extended also to me. My sins were forgiven because I asked Him and I meant it. I am on to new seasons. I am in the prime of my life and I am almost finished with a goal to be a college graduate. But sometimes, just when you have come up for air your life yet again takes a sharp turn at the hands of your decisions. I am single, a college graduate and in the process of obtaining my masters and I'm about to find out exactly what the casualties of my sins really mean. So what do I mean by that? You will soon find out.

I Am Strong, Bold, Beautiful & Free

Casualty of Sin: Chapter 3

I am now 25 years old and in the prime of my life. It seemed at 25 everyone was settling down around me. All my friends were having kids and many were in relationships. Why is this my story? Why am I still single and childless? Is there something wrong with me? These were some of the questions that rang through my head. Truth is it was never an issue of getting a man but keeping him was the struggle. I would come to find out that I was searching for love in all the wrong places. I had failed relationships after failed relationships. It seemed as one was leaving another one was already lurking in the background. As I sit and type this I now know it was a trick of the enemy. I was set up. At that time I was going to church and listening to what the preacher said but never really believing those things would ever apply to me. The seeds were being planted for the day they would spring up and the enemy knew it.

I received Jesus Christ as my Savior after hearing a message of heaven or hell. I think the message scared me so bad that I ran to Jesus not really knowing why or even who He was for that matter. It stirred something up in me to find out what this was all about. I was going to church with my best friend from high school. I wasn't raised in the church but it seemed fun. That day I gave my life to the Lord is a day I will never forget. I remember the first book of the bible I ever read was

Revelation. I read it over the entire weekend at my mom's house when I was visiting her. So I had an introduction to God and was going to church but always felt a void.

I met my daughter's father on what seemed like a prince charming situation. He was much older than me but we fell in love overnight. Well I thought it was love. It went from introduction to engaged in months and pregnant in less than six months! I thought this is perfect! I am finally where I should be, in love and having a baby! He was a gentleman, kind and considerate. He was nothing like anyone I ever dated. He was stable in his life and I was stable, I think. I had just graduated from college and had my own place and my own money. I landed a good job working in housing and would be able to travel a bit doing it. Yeah, this life was going to be nice. My hero came to visit me and took me shopping and treated me amazing. I finally feel loved. I had dated others who I thought I loved but they hurt me and lied to me and after all those psych classes in college I realized that wasn't love but a mind game. So it was perfect. I told him that before I would leave the state and move with him I have to be engaged.

One day I woke up, almost five months pregnant and realized I don't even know this man. I don't even know myself and truth be told who is this baby growing inside of me? I was so lost and alone. I was in a place of isolation just drowning in my own thoughts. So I decided to do what I knew best. I ran. I woke up that morning and told him it's over. I don't have an explanation or even an understanding but I am moving on. I pray that this baby that is growing inside of me will love me and know I don't know what I am doing but I am going to do my best. Just that quickly I was on my own again. This time there was a life inside of me. She needed me. I knew she was my baby girl before it was even confirmed. I always wanted a mini me but didn't realize the depth of what that really meant. Now I have an 11 year old mini me that makes me eat my words lol.

I have always fought for my mini me. I always felt that no matter what mistakes I make in her life she will never be able to say that I didn't fight. We had our first battle at one of our 2nd trimester checkups. I was alone, as usual, when the doctors told me it looks like she has downs syndrome. She is missing a nose and has water on the back of her neck which is a clear indication. They told me I could terminate the pregnancy in Georgia at this stage if I wanted to. Oh, did I fail to tell you all I moved from Connecticut to Florida and then to Georgia all in the matter of months at this time? Yeah I was going through. Always trying to find Jermika but never really could. The doctors sent me home with literature and some options and all I could say on my ride home is Jesus I need you...... What will you have me to do......? As to be expected the Lord came through! He showed me He still loved me even when I didn't love myself. He healed my glimmer of hope as she grew in my womb. He was showing me even back then that He heard my prayers and no good thing would He withhold from me. On November 12, 2005 my baby girl entered the world. I was in love instantly. She belonged to me and no one could ever take her love from me. There were some lonely nights and some hard days. I remember feeling many times I didn't envision it to be like this. Being a single mother was not on my list of goals, but it is what it is.

As my baby grew older I noticed she had trouble connecting and she cried an awful lot. Why is my love not giving me love? It felt more like pain. The only one who I felt could really love me, does not seem to love me. She needs me but doesn't love me. I know now that was the trick of the enemy.

She was diagnosed by doctors at 3 years old with Autism and ADHD. I thought I would feel better knowing what we were dealing with. I was always a problem solver and if we knew the problem I could definitely start chopping away at resolving it. It wasn't as easy as I thought it would be. Truth be told, it was the most challenging thing in my life. It was the beginning of where I found myself in my process of deliverance. As my faith was tested and exercised along the way I would have moments of pure hopelessness. I didn't understand this beautiful gift from God and she did not understand me. I yelled and cried more than I loved and hugged. I was in a fog. I just knew it was punishment from God. I knew that what I felt about my prince charming and this wanted pregnancy was not in alignment with God's will. Oh was I wrong. The very thing that I thought was a punishment was the key to my redemption. I remember one day driving to one of our daily appointments for specialized pre-schooling. I was determined to make my baby girl's life the best it could be. I brought her to the best specialist and spent all I had to use the best holistic methods of treatment. She would do well if I had anything to do with it. So I was driving to pick her up and bring her to the next appointment when I realized I was tired. As I drove over that bridge going 80 miles an hour to get her to her appointments on my 1 hour lunch break....I broke. I wanted to just end the misery that had become my life. I was alone, desperate for rest and desperate for an answer. I yelled out to God, "Why?!".... in the midst of my tears I heard a voice say to me "as you walk I will heal her...."I had never heard that voice before. It startled me. I don't know how I knew it was God but I knew for the first time I recognized His voice. He said it again, "as you walk I will heal her". I literally asked Him what does this have to do with me. I heard nothing. It seems from that moment forward my ears were open to God. I was hearing from Him in all areas of my life. I must admit it did not always bring me comfort. The Lord would speak to me regarding direction and most times inconceivable truth. He began to speak to me and show me why all these things were transpiring in my life. There were roots to these things. There were strongholds in my life that were deeply rooted from a child. I didn't know, no one knew. No one knew how I buried the disappointments of life and it became roots of rejection. No one, not even myself knew that I felt abandoned. While God was dealing with me I kept deflecting back to my baby girl. God I am praying about her not me, why do I keep coming up? I now can hear God's direction for my life and ultimately the answers to my hearts prayers, but at that time, I was in sin. God would constantly remind me as you walk I will heal her. Who can heal autism God? That is what the doctors say. They say therapy will bring forth the best quality of life and I am getting her the best services so I am walking right? I would literally ask these questions to God and His constant answer would be, as you walk I will heal her. I became so frustrated at times because I wanted a new answer. I wanted an answer that made sense to me. What is this walking all about that you want me to do Lord? I went back to the source.

I remembered the days I would go to church when I first got saved and they spoke about a God who heals, delivers and sets free. Let me go back to that place. At that point in my life I was attending church whenever it crossed my mind to go. Truth be told I was going on autopilot. It was the right thing to do. At that time life was good. I was a college graduate, had my three year old daughter and I met a new man. He had been around for a while but we were living together and things were going well. Why not add church into the mix? I would get up and go to church by myself on Sunday mornings. I figured I would go find out what this voice I was hearing was all about and I remembered He is in the house of God. I left my baby home because it was easier, truth be told my boyfriend loved my princess like his very own, it was cool. So I was on a hunt to find out what the walking it out would entail. I didn't realize I was compartmentalizing every circumstance in my life. My daughter's issues were addressed by doctors, my home structure was being addressed by my live in boyfriend and the voice of the Lord I will address at church. Going to service became a regular for me again. It had been years since I was this consistent. When I would go to service it was as if though I never left. The music was awesome and the word was cool. It was uplifting and I felt better for a little while but I still went home with the same issues and questions. I decided I am going to keep going until

I find out what it was that God wanted from me. It was now two years since my baby's diagnosis. She was now five years old and things were getting better but the issues were still daunting. We continued to have parent teacher meetings, after school social groups and me working hard to fix it all! I can't lie and say there 'weren't times I wanted to just give up. I thought why me....? I hated even having those thoughts because I loved her but truth be told I just didn't understand her. Why couldn't she be perfect like me? That was the funny part, perfect like me? I was a hot mess! I can barely stay focused on one thing at a time. I constantly make an 11 day journey turn into 40 years and my idea of love is tainted. Perfect... yeah right. I had some strongholds in my life that haunted me since I was a kid. No one ever knew because I didn't express it much. There was something inside of me that kept me strong when others my age I think, would have broken. Over my life it was easy to not get hurt by others because I just refused to attach myself to things or anyone. I was present but not really present.

Now, here is this little girl looking at me, who has my eyes and looks just like me. She has my heart somehow and to detach myself from her is not possible, so as usual I figured I would fix it! If I could just fix the way she thinks, the way she talks, the difference I see with other children, all will be well. I can fix this! I am a fixer. It seemed the more I tried to fix it the worse things seem to get. Family and friends kept telling me she will grow out of these behaviors. Many couldn't accept the diagnosis of ADHD and Autism. They thought I was overreacting. I was engulfed by this cloud over my head and wanted so badly to heal the one I loved from the womb. I knew what she needed and I was going to solve this issue like I have solved all the other issues I've ever faced.

One day I went to church and they announced we were going on a women's retreat. It sounded like fun, it was something I had never done before. I knew most of the women at my church and I am on a hunt to find out what God is saying to me and why. So before I could talk myself out of not spending the money or going somewhere with "church folks" I signed up. I wasn't concerned about what they thought of me. So what I have a live in boyfriend. So what I like to drink here and there and live my life. I am almost 30 years old and I've been on my own forever. I wish they would say something! You see, I was living this bold undercover life! That sounds like an oxymoron doesn't it? I walked with such a pride that made people not even consider asking me about my personal life. On the other hand I was so sneaky and ashamed of my lifestyle that I did a good job of hiding all the details. Don't forget, I received salvation at 14 years old, so I knew what the word said. I knew what I was doing and the lifestyle I was living was contrary to what I was professing. I was professing salvation, a life for Christ. I was holy.. I think. Either way I was on my way to this retreat.

On April 17, 2010 my life would forever change. I don't remember why I got in that prayer line but I was there. I was ready to find out what God wanted from me. There was something in the atmosphere that I never felt before. My heart became so sorrowful. I was experiencing what I now have come to know as repentance. The woman of God laid hands on me and I felt as if though something mighty pushed me to the ground! I felt something leave me and then something enter me. There was pure peace in that moment. It was just me in that room and God. My mouth began to utter words that were not making sense. I was shaking uncontrollably as it felt like surges were entering me. I was being filled with something but I didn't know what. The next day I was ready to go face the world. I felt like a change had come over me. The preacher kept asking me on our way home, do you realize what just happened. I told her yes, but had no clue! I think I know what has happened but I have a feeling I am about to find out the truth. The things I used to be seemed to have transformed in my mind from a scarlet letter to a place of victory in 24 hours. You see, I had some skeletons…. Although I felt transformed, when I pulled up to my house, I realized something. Nothing had changed at all. My daughter was still struggling, my live in boyfriend was still there and then I had another issue, there was a man on the side that I knew meant me no good. But it still seemed so good. There were casualties in this warzone. People and my family were directly affected by the choices I made whether they were good or bad. God is a forgiver of sins but the reality is there are repercussions for the choices we make. But thank God all things work together for the good of them that love God, and to those who are called according to His purpose. Romans 8:28.

Silly Woman Laden with Sins: Chapter 4

So I returned home apparently transformed on the inside but life is still the same on the outside. It came to me that I had been filled with the Holy Spirit. God had been separating me and my live-in boyfriend for months now. It was just time for us to call it quits. There was no argument, no dispute, no nothing it was just goodbye. He was an amazing man but there was more God wanted from me and this journey was going to have to be solo... So I thought. As soon as I had a clear mind, here comes what seemed to me to be perhaps my husband! I thought wow God you know how to do a quick work. This man came into my life just as quickly as the departure of my live in boyfriend. He definitely was against the grain for me but he intrigued me with the word of God. He fit every physical attribute I desired in a man also. So he knows the word and I am attracted, this has got to be him. He was always kind of around but for some reason we became very fond of each other. I remember one time he told me "you will fall in love alone". You would think after hearing something like that that a sister would walk away. This should have been identified as my way of escape. I was in a trap that the scripture warned me of. 2 Timothy 3, was my life written in a nutshell at this point. So what do you think I did at this point? Instead of turning away, I was determined to make this man love me. He just didn't know he wanted it yet. When he finally saw all that I was, he would want me. So you would think I knew my worth if I figured in my mind that a man couldn't resist all that I had and even all that I was. I was smart, attractive, had my own home and a fabulous career. What is there not to love? I now realize I put so much weight onto material things and my physical features that the very core of who I was, was ugly and dying. The enemy was cunning but my God is greater. You see what the devil meant for bad God always meant for good. I was setting sail for a web of deception. I mistook his being a lover of himself for confidence and even his form of godliness for truth. It is strange how some things can appear so clear but when the flesh is engaged the mind becomes so cloudy. I had just come out of a relationship that God required of me only to run into what became a spiritual nightmare. I got caught up in a whirlwind of sin. I was torn between God and the flesh. Out of the same mouth would come the word of the Lord but then that same midnight call of WYD would come? You all know that call. That what are you doing call in the deep of the night. So now I am stuck! God is telling me to walk and my daughter will be healed, my flesh is on fire and I am learning how to exegete the word of God at the same time! Pure confusion….. God is not the author of confusion, so something had to give. I wanted to break free from it all. I wanted to break free from the responsibilities of a mom, for being accountable to the church, for saying yes to God, I just wanted to live on the wild side for a minute. That is exactly what I did. This woman of God would have these sexual escapades with this man of God. It's amazing how the world can see you as a totally different person than you really are. I often thought if people truly walked in discernment we would be so exposed. I knew it wouldn't last long. There was a tugging on my heart every time I fell. I got tired of repenting. God began to speak to me in different ways than before. I didn't hear that same voice on the inside anymore. I would have these dreams and visions of the rapture, death, hidden treasures and sin. I remember having a dream where I was ashamed to look up. I was laying at Jesus's feet. I could see his feet and he was calling my name and telling me to look up. I just couldn't do it. People around me were being raptured but the shame was holding me down. Finally at the final hour I got the courage to take heed to his call and looked up and he took me. It was just a dream but I was being warned and being called to repentance. I had the Holy Spirit now down on the inside so it hurt me to sin against God but my flesh was still in control. God was calling my name to get it right. I would sometimes ask for forgiveness in advance of my sins to soften the blow. Now today I know that is Ludacris. We can't bank on tomorrow's mercy. God forbid. There were so many warnings from the Lord during this uncomely rendezvous. Sickness even begin to occur in my body. The doctors would tell me they weren't sure what was going on and I would hear the Lord tell me to stop sinning for it was affliction. WHAT DO YOU WANT FROM ME?? I felt like I was damned if I did and damned if I didn't. My baby wasn't getting better and I am unhappy. So the war in my body went on for months. This man had no intention of marrying me. Let alone he had no intentions of dating me. We would have these momentous occasions where I would think he finally saw my worth but he would remind me in his actions that it was not so. The truth is, how can someone find their worth when they themselves don't know it. I was filled with the precious gift of the Holy Spirit but my mind had not been made up. I was living with strongholds from my childhood and young adult life that constantly spoke defeat to me. So walking with an unsteady mind and sleeping with a man with his own demons what do you expect to happen? How is that possible? There can only be one master in our lives and my free will was still intact. I chose to let my flesh lead. I was on this up and down journey of trying to find out who I was and what I wanted and yet my baby girl is still in need of healing. The crazy thing is that in this toxic lust- filled agreement I found out more about God. When we weren't lusting after each other we actually studied. He gave me study guides and tips he had learned about the bible. I learned how to thoroughly exegete the scripture through our studies. The truth is God will use even the areas of sin you decide to live in for His good. He will take the good that is being presented and safeguard it for when you are fully converted. God knew I would come out of this. I was studying beyond Sunday services now. I was intrigued by what was being revealed to me in the word. He was becoming real to me. God is real and He wants something from me. Again…. Lord what do you want from me? The more I would read the more unattractive my agreement with this man became. I keep calling it an agreement because that is what it was. To call it a relationship is delusional. I wanted out but my flesh was on fire. The more I would hear the word and write sermons on the back of receipts and any paper I could find, it told me there is something different about me. I began to pray more and more for relationship with God. The dreams continued and I began to realize it was God speaking to me in new ways. They were God given dreams. Then one day everything changed…… I invited him over as usual. We were on the verge of becoming intimate and I saw a light. The whole room lit up and I was exposed. I felt the presence of God himself and He was not pleased with me. The level of conviction I felt made me scream out as this man was rounding 3rd base! He jumped up and stared at me for a moment. I cried like I had never cried before. It was a cry from my soul. My father was in the room. He was looking at me in all my filth and sin. I felt the shame of disgracing my Lord and Savior. The man I was with left out the room and it felt like I cried for hours. I felt as if though he had seen my heavenly father standing there too. When I got myself together the light was gone but I felt free! I felt like this life I had been living was now truly dead. I had to go face this man and tell him this is over…. As I slowly walked down the stairs wondering what do I say, what do I do, I didn't have to say a word. The man I had been sleeping with and learning about God with, turned to me and said "I can't do this anymore". He said you are special to God. It feels like I am sleeping with a married woman when I am with you. And just like that it was all over. There was no heartache, no back and forth or let's try to make it work. No, it was over. Gifts begin to stir up in me from that moment of liberation. I was focused on being obedient to God and on my continued search to find out what my walk would consist of. I would hear things in the Spirit about others, I would feel the pain of a woman as I walked past her in the supermarket. I would begin to pray for relief of the pain I was feeling and in turn they were feeling. I was learning I was called to intercession. I was beginning to see the gifts that were in me before my mother's womb. It scared me. Things are moving too fast. What do you mean you are calling me to do this work? I feel like I just walked out of the hospital myself and you are sending me to set the captives free? I was back to a new screaming match with God! Truth be told it was very one- sided. I am now alone again with a child in need of healing and in an empty house and spiritual things are happening. God's answer remained the same, as you walk I will heal her.

In 2012 I was ready to try something new. My mind was clear and I and my home girl were single Christian women on a hunt to find out what our purposes were. I learned to step out of the boat. Actually I dove into the water head first. I needed change, I needed a new experience. We both were in a place of hurt and pain and were on the road to recovery. One day I saw a TD Jakes commercial for Woman Thou Art Loosed I told my homegirl we should and my mother too. We made a quick decision to do it and we were off. As we traveled all the way to Atlanta I knew there was something waiting there for me. My mom and I were also on a journey together of getting to know each other a little deeper. Old wounds were in the process of being mended. It would be like pulling off an old scab with one shot but it was necessary to let healing truly begin. So let's go!! I needed God in the worst way. There were too many open doors that needed to be shut so that new ones could be presented. Walking into an arena with 20,000 women, looking for the same God but for different things was life changing. I didn't know their stories but we were all the same. We were hungry. We wanted out. I wondered if they could hear the same voice I was hearing and having the same type of dreams I was having. I remember the message TD Jakes preached. He preached, "The Pecking Order". I remember repeating amongst all those women, "Position, Exposure, Courage and Knowledge!" I was pecking my way out of the prison I was held in. I had questions I needed answers to and I wasn't going home until I got them. I screamed "Lord I came all the way to Atlanta to hear what you really want from me and finally I got my answer!" You see, it wasn't that He wasn't speaking, I just had selective hearing. There was a point where I couldn't hear anything, but saw the Holy Spirit racing across the multitude of women and He was heading straight for me. A fresh wind was about to hit me and I knew something was about to happen. Boom... I saw a mirror. A woman standing there and it was me. She was broken in many pieces. He told me "I am washing you and I am sending you. You will be used by me." He took His hand and touched me from head to toe. I felt the hand of God cleaning me all over again. I wept and screamed for joy. I knew I was yet again forgiven. I sat down and collected myself and it was as if a switch was turned back on in my ear. I heard the Lord say, "Listen, I am about to tell you who I am sending you to." During that conference a woman stood up and began to talk to us about something I never heard of. She asked how many of you are familiar with sex trafficking? Those words went straight from her mouth and into my heart. He told me that He is sending me to the lost. I wondered, am I not lost? But now I know who I am walking toward. She has a name. Her name is Lost. I wrote it down in 2012, a woman formally laden with sins was being sent to set the captives free. I had no idea what it would look like, but I knew I was equipped with power and a new understanding of who God was and therefore who He called me to be.

The invaluable Self Worth: Chapter 5

At this point, I loved to study the word of God and even felt like He was calling me to be a minister. So I began taking classes at the church for aspiring ministers. I felt so unworthy to be there. Look what I just came out of. Why would God want me to minister His word? I knew God's voice although I ignored it many times. He told me to get in the class so I did. One day I was speaking with a girl friend of mine about all that had transpired. She was encouraging me to keep pursuing God. I had an "Ah Ha" moment when speaking with her. I told her that I don't know how to love myself. I confessed that I feel unworthy to be loved by anyone. No one has ever loved me. Now whether that was true or not, it was how I felt. I confessed that I had never been without a man in my adult life. That I was always chasing love and it never showed up. From that conversation with her that day, I prayed to the Lord and meant it. I was afraid to say it but I needed it. I asked the Lord to show me what love was and how to be content with only Him in my life. My prayer was answered instantaneously. There was no distraction for years. No one called, no one sent a "wyd" (What you doing) text or even asked me for my phone number. It was as if a veil was put over me. You would think I would be happy about my prayer being answered, but it was unfamiliar. Have you ever noticed how even a dysfunctional situation can be acceptable just because it's familiar? Where were the men? Was I no longer attractive? I was about to surely find out what it meant to be invaluable. To be invaluable meant to understand that the true level of my worth exceeded what I ever thought of myself. I never had time to truly look at myself from the inside out. I was so accustomed to looking at myself from the outside in. My exterior self would dictate how I felt. I would adorn myself with the sexiest clothing I could find. The more skin the better! It got me so much attention. Subconsciously, I thought if I could just reel them in they would come to love the stock of who I was. I was no dumb woman. I was driven to succeed. My beauty would captivate them and then they would come to fall in love with my personality, my drive and my over the top sense of humor. It never happened that way. The same man with a different face approached me every time and never got past the tube top and the short shorts. But now it's dead silent. What do I do now? I feel like there is so much idle time. I would pray more and more for understanding of what was to come. I jumped into this cold turkey. I said to be alone means I declare celibacy right? What in the world is celibacy? I have been having sex since I was 14. How can I turn back the hands of time and say RESET? I made the declaration to be alone with God for however long He needed me to without asking Him how long and what was it going to cost me. It began with long days and lonely nights. The silence can be so loud when there are no distractions to life. God began to show me the reality of my world and who I had become. It was ugly. I was living in a place of resentment and bitterness. I was walking around like a robot on auto pilot. I woke up, got my daughter to school, went to work, studied the word and prayed and went to bed. It was a routine. I was emotionless and going through the motions. I provided for my daughter's needs physically, and ensured her protection, obtained services for the disability and all, but I was lacking something. I couldn't figure out what it was. I was no longer engulfed in the lust of the flesh, so I figured this is what life was. We were finally living the life God wanted us to live. I became very complacent. The bills were being paid and my daughter was making great strides in school, socially and academically. Life is great! It was an illusion. I was putting makeup on a cracked face and just patching the holes as I went. I wasn't interested in going deeper. So I pressed on and felt that if God wants to deal with it, He will. Until then, we will continue on autopilot, it's safer. Thank God I had an awesome girlfriend that I conversed with regularly or I may have lost it totally in this season of my life. Nothing looked the same. My life was no longer dysfunctional, but at least the dysfunction was a part of my normalcy.

My girlfriend and I hung out and did a lot of things together to keep ourselves busy. She was the first woman I felt vulnerable enough to talk to. I was in a very lonely place but knew I needed help. I didn't know who I was and it was beyond uncomfortable. Talk about feeling worthless. I knew God said I had value, but everything I ever valued in myself was no longer engaged. My wardrobe changed, my thoughts changed and my friends changed. One day I decided to slowly let down the walls that I thought protected me because I had the ability to do so. It was a strange ability. I could resurrect and tear down this wall around my heart at any given moment, but truth be told it was a prison. That wall told me to only go this far, or the wall is being ambushed, build it higher. I no longer wanted to protect myself though. For once in my life I wanted to feel true emotions and love. I wanted to be protected by the Lord. I was learning scripture each and every day. I was reading the words that He was my strong tower, my rock, and my fortress. I want Him to guard my heart because I have come to find out my tactics aren't working. I'm smiling and it's fake. I am saying I love you to my daughter and it seems shallow. I wanted to know my worth, I wanted to know her worth. God said I am worth more than rubies but I felt like a cubic zirconia. I could be set in real gold, but over time my sparkle and shine would wear off because it wasn't real. I never felt quite real.

For many years, I would evolve to fit who ever I was with or who I was talking to. I would make up stories in my head about myself and my life to first make myself believe it and then try to make others believe it too. I was tired of this fantasy world and I was ready to offer my reasonable service...holiness. I didn't really have a mentor in my life at that time. There were many women in the church that I would take note of and watch. I would take pieces of their lives and try to apply it to my life and ask, is this holiness?

While I was on my journey of trying to fix this area of my life, God was already working on the inside. He wrote the story. He knew my journey and I began to realize the battle was not mine but the Lord's. He was stirring on the inside of me. I would speak with my girlfriend about my issues in life. I told her how I didn't trust anyone and how I wanted more. We would talk for hours at times and encourage one another. She was in a process too. We were both looking and seeking God for something. We knew there was more. So each and every day I would seek His face. I would read His word and receive so much revelation. I was in a school of one. I didn't speak much to anyone inside of the church. I didn't share this experience with anyone pretty much, other than her. What if I fail at this? I don't want anyone to know my issues and my struggles. Let them continue to see the smiling face and bodily exercise I give on Sundays. I would shout and dance but truly had no song. It was rough trying to kill my flesh. I was used to a touch that would put the fire out but there was no more quenching of the fire. My body begin to rage up and I didn't know what to do. I had been filled with the Holy Ghost, but now, I know I had yet to fully submit to Him. It was as if I invited Him in and showed Him no hospitality. I ignored Him. I didn't even acknowledge Him. I didn't ask Him for His help to keep me. I needed a solution to kill this flesh because I still kept it alive and well. Ok God... am I walking yet? Do you see this sacrifice I'm making? It's been a few months, have I done what you needed me to do yet?

I asked a friend what I could do and she recommended masturbation. I was like I never really tried that, but I needed something in order that I might not fall. I wanted to be kept you see. I wanted to see the healing that God promised me. So I made a move! I purchased a sex toy that rocked my world! It was great! My flesh was being kept and my hands were being kept clean, so I thought. My sister in Christ used this technique to keep her and she seemed pretty grounded so this has got to work for me. I was being kept by what they called "The Rabbit", but I still didn't see much change in my life. I came to find out the hard way my celibacy was a default, it was a fake. There was no one around to entice me but this rabbit I controlled. I would soon find out the struggle of not fully submitting to the will of God. I began chasing Christian conference after Christian conference to get my mind off my raging hormones. At these conferences, I would have these momentous occasions. I would hear the Lord tell me I was beautiful, how much He loved me and how valuable I was to Him. I never believed him. I would think how am I beautiful and no man wants me? How do you love me, when I have faced so many things growing up and have a child with a disability on my own? How can you really say you love me? Then you tell me I am valuable, but yet I struggle to even love myself.

I've felt abandoned at times, always a secondary figure in other people's lives. So many times I left the conference angrier at the self-revelations than the experience. But hey, I had the rabbit to fall back on! Until one day I spoke with another sister of mine. I will tell you more about her later but I was in "the store" that hosted my friend the rabbit, when she called me. You see, when touching things you are truly not supposed to, you will always be on the chase to find the next greatest high. It is like a gateway drug and you're always chasing the experience. I was in this store creeping and dodging hoping no one saw this aspiring minister in a sex shop, when my phone rang. My sister asked me repeatedly where I was. I would answer her by saying "out and about, chilling". She knew something was up. Then she said to me, "Don't buy it." She said, "It's time to kill that flesh. You are having sex with a toy, not a man but it is still wrong in God's eyes." The flesh was still winning and God was not able to move in my life when I allowed the flesh to lead. My free will was surely intact and the flesh was winning. I ignored her advice and thanked her. You see, my other Christian friend told me it was ok and I saw her life which appeared to be fruitful. I think I will bank on the evidence. So I purchased my new friend and went home. On the way home I kept thinking about the item and what my friend had just said to me. When I got home, I decided to take my new toy for a test drive. As soon as I took it out of the package, I heard that voice again that I heard when I drove across that bridge before. He said, "throw it away!" When I heard that familiar voice I began to weep. I told Him I just paid my last $80.00 for this! He asked me if I trusted Him. I don't remember if I answered or not. He told me to throw it all away and to let Him keep me. I knew He meant business. I knew something was about to happen in my life. I was about to go in that deeper place that I desired, but feared to go. I picked up all the toys I had and threw them in the garbage. I called up my friend who advised me to throw them away and told her all that has happened. We rejoiced on the phone and praised God. See there was something different about her. There was something different about me. We both wanted to find out what this invaluable self-worth was all about. We were beyond just someone's daughter, someone's mother but there was a purpose in our lives and we were about to find out what it was.

The Call: Chapter 6

It is now time to explore life. I am in a place of true surrender, to the Holy Spirit who is now within me. I feel like a fresh wind has come over me. I am finally learning what true intimacy feels like. The purging process is still continuing, but it is a day by day and moment by moment process. I am no longer feeling so overwhelmed by the lust and shame, but I am being refined. I still feel a little edgy, not as cut to the pattern of most of the church women I see. Regardless, I am falling in love with God. I have an amazing mentor in my life who pours into me spiritually and naturally. Things could not be any better. My daughter is making leaps and bounds in school and is socially growing. We still have our growing pains, but there is a peace there that I just don't know how to describe. I began getting busy in the church. I was working in leadership in the church and with the national church doing the work of the Lord.

I remember walking through the basement of the church with my mentor and other members of the church. We had just finished up an intense meeting where God showed up. He used me to speak a word in the meeting. I didn't understand how the voice I heard, was now using my mouth to speak His words. I remember speaking a word of correction and before I could even hold back it was being said. I remember feeling overwhelmed at what had just happened. It was my first time knowingly being used by God to speak His revelation. My mentor sensed this transition in me and began to pray over me. Before I knew it, she and I were on the floor. I was drenched in His presence. I remember the Lord using her to say to me "You are going to lead His people". I was overwhelmed with grief. Yes, I said grief. What do you mean I am going to lead His people? I don't want to do that. I am comfortable just living a life holy unto Him. Just sitting in the third pew from the front and working casually in the church. I knew what she said was true though. Although it happened years ago, I remember it like it was yesterday. Is this finally what He meant when He told me that as I walk my baby will be healed? The very thought of it scared me.

Confirmation and revelation is all that followed me from that point. Along the way, something is also happening between my new friend and I when it comes to ministry. We are being accountable to one another and vulnerable. The vulnerability made me cringe at first. I am not use to telling someone else my deepest secrets and greatest fears. I was used to moving in silence. It was easier that way. I was used to no one telling me about myself or advising me in any way. We were both so hungry for God that we were willing to trust each other, in order to find out what He put in us. We were going through a major metamorphic experience. She was changing and I was changing and it seemed at microwave speed. We read and studied the word of God together. Most of our conversations were more about Jesus than anything else. I was so thankful for this new found friendship and accountability. There were many sisters I had in my life in the past, but never one like her. She was probably one of the only people who told me straight truth about myself. She didn't sugar coat it, but informed me of my shortcomings and followed it up by encouraging me with the word. So with all this goodness going on I knew I was bound to find out that there was more. I was no longer hearing from the Lord once in a while. His voice became constant to me. When I would open up His word, I would see words highlighted on the page. I couldn't wait to dissect the words and see what else He wanted to show me. I found myself having conversations with this invisible God out loud. I could hardly focus on anything else. I would be sitting in service on Sundays, hearing the sermon and unable to keep up because I heard a word in his message. I began writing messages on the back of receipts when I was driving in my car because I heard God speak. God was drawing me in deeper and deeper. I remember sitting at service and hearing the announcement that the aspiring ministers class was going to start. The voice of the Lord said "Get there." So my response was,"Why? First my mentor tells me I am going to lead the people and now you tell me to get into the aspiring ministers class? All I have ever been looking for was relationship with you and wholeness for my daughter was what I thought. That is not my thing. Do you remember who I was and what I have done? I am not the "preaching type." God reminded me every day leading up to that class to show up. I enjoyed the class immensely. I was learning about the very things that were happening to me spiritually. Is this it Lord? You have called me to preach your word? Ok, I guess I can do this. Before I knew it sermons were flowing out of me. I never anticipated on preaching any way. God just told me to get in the class so I did. Years went by and I was still in the class, enjoying it just as I did on the first day.

It is now 2014 and I am in the prime of my life. I am hearing from God, I am in an aspiring minister's class and I am in the midst of the church's annual Daniel fast. I decided to try this fasting. This was the first time I really would try to stick to 21 days of no meats and no sweets. What are you doing Jermika? God didn't say you had to do this. I believed what my Pastor spoke about fasting and praying. I believed there was yet still more I was about to find out, so I dove in. My flesh was literally dying. I relied so heavily on the Holy Spirit that from sunup to sundown I woke up speaking to Him. I was taken in deeper than I could ever imagine. God told me I was being sent. Sent where? He would test my obedience with requiring me to go after things beyond my comprehension. Where are you sending me to I would ask? My answer would be a new task or requirement. During this time the Lord spoke to me and my accountability partner (sister) and said start a ministry called Who Art Thou My Daughter Ministry. We both heard the Lord and had no idea what this meant. We just knew that when the two of us met each other we were being sent two by two and we became free. It was now our turn to lead our sisters to freedom. We had no idea what we were doing. We relied on God for every detail. I have to say, when you rely on God at that magnitude you cannot fail. Here were two women who have recently been delivered, belonging to two different churches, and now establishing a ministry. How in the world did we get here? Our first event was amazing. It was January 11, 2014. Woman came and fellowshipped. We cried, we laughed and we opened up to one another. It was one of the most amazing moments of my life. I finally felt I belonged to something amazing. My hands were producing something that was going to change lives and didn't come from my own strength. God gave us every detail and every idea that He wanted to see happen and they were blessed. I don't know who was blessed more, the ladies or my sister and I.

So we are now walking in a ministry of healing that would eventually evolve into... a ministry of deliverance. I was so busy working in the Lord, that I didn't have time to get caught up in idle mischief. It felt so good to be doing something positive and productive. I had a good job and life was good. I knew there were about to be transitions taking place in my life, but they would be for the good. I was always a creature of habit, and change was not invited but I recognized it was necessary. I'm walking in this new call on my life to bring my sisters to a place of healing. We were called to bring them to an atmosphere and understanding of where and who Christ was, and He would do the rest. I felt so strong in the Lord. He is continuing to deliver me even as I allow Him to use me to deliver them.

One day, my sister and I decided to go on a trip. We decided to get out of our comfort zones and start going on road trips and to conferences. We went to conferences down south, locally and wherever the Lord led us. We found out so many things we didn't know about ourselves and our gifts. I found out that I truly walk in prophetic ministry and I also had a gift of administration. There was so much more that I would come to find out that He put in me but I'll save it for later. Those two things were enough to make me pause and take a break.

I remember taking a road trip to Maryland in 2015. We were heading to a conference hosted by Dr. Jazz

Sculark. I remember driving in the car with such great expectation. We were getting revelation after revelation heading down that highway! I remember feeling so nervous about going to a place and being amongst people we did not know. All we knew were each other but we needed to go and explore life outside of our bubbles. I remember going into worship and the Lord using my sister to lay hands on me and declare a word of "Mending a matter of my heart". I didn't even realize I had matters of the heart until I felt God's presence literally rest on my heart and begin to do surgery. The peace I felt was again on another level of experience. It was like our relationship became sweeter and sweeter. I found that as I desired and step out into the unknown, the more fear would try to stop me from going beyond the comfort zone. I received my life's liberation scripture at that conference in Maryland. The moderator asked all the women to choose a scripture that will allow them to always remember that they are free. I randomly opened my bible and said God show me. My finger landed on Romans 8:30; "Moreover whom he did predestinate, them He also called, and whom He called, them He also justified and whom He justified them He also glorified." This became my mantra. I have never been one to be able to quickly memorize scripture or anything for that matter. Memorization took great effort for me. However, the more intimate I became with God and relied on the Holy Spirit, the more He would bring all things back to my remembrance. With this new responsibility on my life at times I have to remind myself that He predestined me. I didn't ask Him for it, He put it inside of me before I was even conceived. Then at the appropriate time He called me. He called me forward and asked me if I would allow Him to use me. It is hard to resist the request of your redeemer, your deliverer and the lover of your soul. Then to know that He justified me... My God. Coming into a knowing of who God called me to be, created great areas of doubt and unworthiness. I wondered what people would think and what they would say. Who am I to be used of God in this way? He has to grab and shake me out of it sometimes even to this day and He says "I justified you". Justified is past tense. It has already been spoken that there is a call on my life, so God let it be so. Then to top it all off, He tells me that He glorified me. It is His glory that man sees. I am walking in God's glory but yet it doesn't belong to me it belongs to Him. He humbles me and keeps me in constant reverence, to the point that people see him and not me. I honor His presence in my life and will not take for granted the very fact that I stand amongst the called.

The Art of War: Chapter 7

I am now a spiritual soldier in God's army and I am armed and ready for war. One thing I didn't realize is that when much is given, much is required. It is now 2016 and Who Art Thou My Daughter Ministry is in full motion. God has evolved the ministry greatly and told us it will be a ministry of deliverance. What does that even mean? It seemed as if though we found out before the question was fully proposed. I remember having an event for women and at that event a woman showed up with some peculiar behaviors. A minister in the church said this woman needs prayer and demons don't wait. Did she say demons? I know we had been studying about the authority and power that God has given the believer over all the power of the enemy, but I had never seen it up close and personal so I thought. We were in charge that night so we needed to address this. The thing is we were not afraid. We believed God at His word. We prayed with that woman for what seemed like an eternity. From that day forward we realized that the scriptures are true. We wrestle not against flesh and blood but against principalities, against powers, against the rulers of darkness of this world and against spiritual wickedness in high places Ephesians 6:12. I was not afraid but apprehensive. Did I believe He is truly working in me to be able to stand up against the enemy? Little did I realize, I had been in basic training all this time! You see, the things I faced in my life were always spiritual attacks to steal, kill and destroy me. The spirits of lust, perversion, lies, self-doubt, self-sabotage, fear, abandonment, offence and rejection were always after me. I realized they were not only after me but after my daughter and my family too. I couldn't have that. I know way too much. I have seen way too much of God's power to not believe Him for myself and my family. The enemy would creep into my own home and try to disturb the peace in my home. I would have to fight at times, day and night to declare I will not be moved. It was like Pandora's Box had been opened. I would get so tired of fighting sometimes I would just sit and cry to be rescued like David did. I remember coming home from the movie War Room and at 10pm at night emptying out one of the only closets in my small cape house and putting an ottoman, a table and a light in there and saying "This means war". I need my God to fight for me for where He was sending me. My daughter has all of my heart and I was not going to allow the enemy to use her and hurt her. So I learned the art of war in my own home and amongst my own family. The Lord would wake me up in the middle of the night at times and have me walking my house and calling down demonic forces in the name of Jesus. He would show them to me by name and He still does to this day. I remember walking in a room in my home and having a picture of a unicorn on the wall that I put up when we first moved in. The

Lord spoke to me that it had to come down. He showed me the insidiousness of the enemy trying to creep in and required that it be removed. I thought, a unicorn Lord? The next morning my daughter asked me a question about a unicorn wizard that was in the game Pokémon. It was moments like that where I learned not to question God's instruction. We can't afford to question God's instruction when He tells us we are armed for battle. You see, a soldier is only as good as his obedience and armor in war. When many are running out, I am running in. I have had to face the principality of rejection head on. I used to sabotage relationships at the fear of being rejected. Great friendships were lost due to rejection. I saw the trend in the women in my family at the hands of this spirit. I make a stance that no principality has a hold on my family or the generation that is to come from my bloodline. When you start talking in the spirit, people start believing that you're crazy. We have to remember, in warfare there are times that others around you don't realize the enemy is in the midst. You're the one saying, "shhhhhh something is here", and they are telling you that you're overreacting and nothing is there. Trust what God is showing you, so that the moment the enemy attacks, it will be your sword that covers them and you. It is like in those scary movies where there is one girl who says no we shouldn't go there. There is always some bold one that tells her to be quiet and proceeds on, but then there are some that trust that she knows something and sticks with her. In war, no matter if they go or stay it is important that we stay on duty as God has called us. God has shown me to separate the person from the problem. Don't be afraid to call it out and rebuke it and speak life. There are times when I notice an attack of the enemy on myself and on my daughter's mind. She will be afraid to try new things at the risk of failing. She will tell me I don't love her and that I like other people more than her. In those moments, I have to stop, listen and speak. Stop what you're doing and self-analyze. Am I loving the way she needs and deserves to be loved? Am I as present as she needs me to be? Then listen for a response from God. The greatest position to have in war is self-aware. We are all fallible and fall short, but thank God we have a redeeming and delivering Savior. If we can admit our faults and ask Him for His help, He will not only restore all that was effected and tainted, but also teach us and allow us to have a testimony of deliverance. Now it is time to speak. We have to speak out of our mouths. Renounce, rebuke, declare and affirm. I have shared the declarations of God with my daughter many times in calmness and peace. I have said "I rebuke fear and doubt and I speak you are strong and fearless and sure. You are loved and needed and wanted." She has not always understood what I was saying and at times it seemed to frustrate her. But again, separate the person from the problem. Who am I fighting? I am not fighting my daughter, I am not fighting my mother and I am not even fighting myself. I am fighting the enemy of my soul.

I remember taking a trip and a woman sat next to me on the plane. As soon as she sat down I knew she was about to share something with me that was going to change my life forever. She introduced herself and told me she was a happily married woman, with an adult son and traveled the world with her husband who had an amazing career. Her life appeared so carefree to me. I wondered why this woman was sharing all of this with me. Before we were even high above the clouds, she had told me of the amazing life she lived. I'm wondering, God why is she telling me all of this. I looked down at the sparkling diamond on her hand it seemed like her hand was calling for my attention. God began to speak to my heart about where my life was heading and He wanted me to listen. After painting this amazing life to me she asked me if I have children. I told her I have an amazing daughter. She said her son is 21 and is married. But there was a time in her life that she thought he would never make it in life. Now, she really had my attention. She began to tell me that her son had anxiety as a child that crippled him. She said she would cry every day at the thought of having to wake him up and deal with the argument and fear of going to school. It crippled her at just the thought. She loved her son, but hated what he put her through. Just five minutes before I couldn't remotely relate to this upper class, well dressed, at least three carat diamond wearing white woman. Now, all of a sudden she is right on my street. We didn't talk about whether we were Christians just yet, but I know she saw God in me and I was seeing Him in her without even having to announce it. She told me that she grew up catholic, so she didn't really know about spiritual attacks or anything like that, but had enough of their lives being crippled by these anxiety attacks. She said his attacks got worse and worse and she began researching what these attacks could be beyond what the doctors and school psychiatrist were telling her. So, one day, she ran across an online book by Sheryl Brady that said, "Today we fight the spirit of anxiety." It felt like her answer was in that book. She continued to tell me how she learned about Jesus and the power and authority He had given the believer. Then she finished the book and decided today is the day that I am going to teach my son what I have learned. I am going to teach him how to fight. She said she felt so empowered that morning. She didn't cry, she woke him up with expectation that today would be different. She said it was the total opposite. It was one of the worst mornings they ever had. As they sat in the principal's office her son was so filled with fear of everyone looking at him, that it crippled him. As this stranger spoke to me I felt like she was me. I remember those mornings with my baby girl in elementary school. I remember those tears, I remember those fears. Why is this lady walking me through my life right now? As I listened barely breathing and with a frog in my throat, she continued to look me in my eyes and said "I said to my son, David the devil doesn't want you to go to class. He doesn't want you to learn and be confident. No one is looking at you. I need you to tell the devil that you are going to class and fear will no longer hold you back." She said as boldly as it came out of me, my son jumped up, wiped his face and said devil I am going to class! She said her son walked into that class and never looked back. He is now 21 years old with a wife, starting a career and has a new baby. Now she and her husband travel the world and spoil their new grandbaby.

I sat there with tears in my eyes as God just showed me that my life will be full of greatness. That the peace and power He showed her resides in me. She must have sensed my connection because she said, "Jermika, teach her how to fight." It wasn't that lady at all that told me this but it was that voice again from God. I was convinced that every war tactic I was being shown by God, I needed to show my daughter. The enemy is not only after my anointing, but hers as well. From that time forward, I equip my daughter with the word of God every day. I prayed over her at night and asked her to pray over me. She was tired of the prayer assignments and the study sessions at first, but before I knew it, she was speaking even over herself without being prompted.

A woman on a 2 hour flight showed me the next level of strategy that will be needed in this war we are in. We still have battles to this day, but I know that the word of God will always prevail. So we no longer run and we no longer retreat. Instead, we face each giant and know we have a sling and some smooth stones. We call out the giants by name and speak the name of Jesus against them. As attacks come, like anger and resentment, we address them with the same power and authority that we address the others. We are children of the most high God. There is a holy call on our lives and although the weapons form, they shall not prosper. The knowing, is the very beginning of the art of war. The bible says offenses must come, but woe by whom they come. God will deal with every attack, offense, snare and trap of the enemy. He does not leave us ignorant of the enemy's devices. The question is what's in your hand Moses? Jermika, what is in your hand?

I remember being in prayer one day. I was so heavy laden with shame. I felt the attacks were because of what I did. How I yelled at her when she was younger.

How I lacked patience in dealing with her anxieties and lack of communication. I blamed myself and wallowed in shame. God let me complain and speak against myself. When I was finished He said, "What is inside of you? You are a fire starter, you are a warrior, and you are a teacher." I said,"Me? I am ashamed." He said, "You are not ashamed, you are an overcomer. Overcome Jermika. Speak against the wounds and the accusations of the enemy directed at you. Be who I called you to be. What is inside of you Jermika?" My reply was, "You!"

I must say, 2016 was a year of many truths. That time in prayer and the people God was sending to me, told me there is still more in me that needs to come out. I am a soldier fighting with a limp. The limp is stifling me from being as quick and strong and confident as I need to be. I had been dreading this moment for years but it was time to dig. There was a woman of God for years the Lord had been telling me to go and see. She would help me dig up the root of the residue in my life. Before I could talk myself out of it or succumb to the whispers of the enemy, I made the appointment. I remember driving there and telling myself don't say too much just go and listen. When I stepped in her office the presence of God was waiting for me. I am so vulnerable in front of Him and did not like the feeling. I tried my best to resurrect my wall of protection but I couldn't. I couldn't call forward my protection. What protection? God is my protection and He is sitting in my mist. I remember driving home that day in silence. No music, no sound at all. Just my heart beat and deep breaths. As I drove on the highway, I remember having the urge to open my mouth. When I opened my mouth a scream came out of me that scared me. It scared me so bad I began crying heavily and had to pull over. God said I am purging. Let it out. I sat there and let the process happen. When it was all over, peace fell upon me. I felt like I knew it all and she was just being sent to me for confirmation but truth is she helped me dig. She put the shovel in my hand and told me to dig. Each session was just like that. Here is your shovel now dig. That process of exposing and uprooting has brought me to this place today. I envision myself standing on a mountain in full war gear, with a flag in one hand and a weapon in the other. I no longer have tears of anguish, shame and fear. I am standing free of shame, a warrior fit to be used by God. I have completed basic training and I am in the continued process of specialized training. I am called to preach the word of God. I am strong, I am bold, I am beautiful, I am...........

The Promise….. Chapter 8

Free….. I am free. I declare today that the last hurdle of this journey is complete. I am sure there will be more challenges in life I will have to face but I will face them fully equipped. One might ask how I can be so sure. I heard the Lord tell me all is well. I heard the Lord tell me He never left me nor will He ever forsake me. I know Him by name and He knows me. As 2016 ended and 2017 began the Lord required a promise from me. I was at a women's prayer retreat and He required me to share with a group of ladies the call on my life. We were playing a fun game that got very real. God swept the atmosphere and began requiring declarations at that table filled with powerful and anointed young women of God. He reminded me of what He told me on January 14, 2016. I remembered what He said but I didn't understand it. I didn't know what He meant when He touched me and called me by name. He told me Jermika you are my Apostle. I was so afraid to speak it from my mouth because of what I heard and saw an Apostle to be. Isn't that some denomination or something? Why are you calling me that Lord? I left it alone and wrote it down and began to receive confirmation after confirmation. I felt I needed to find out what this call was all about. I didn't want to learn from anyone's dogma or even bench mark off of the mentorship of another Apostle. I went straight into the word of God. I studied the scriptures of what an

Apostle was and is today. I learned that an Apostle is a messenger, a harbinger, one sent of God. Sent with a specific message; a champion of critical reform. This call to present Jesus as the restorer to the survivors of sex trafficking is largely a part of the call on my life. I am being sent into places many don't desire to go and walk in signs in wonders through the power of God that most don't want to lay hands on. I am an Apostle not of men neither by man, but by Jesus Christ and God the father who raised Him from the dead. Gal. 1:1. In prayer God would show me how hard it would be, but to remember that He called me. As I dove deeper into the scriptures to find out what this requirement would be, I asked the Lord to take this cup from me. I was serious. I don't want that mantle on my life. Remember I like sitting in the 3rd row on the left and participating as needed. This is a life's mandate Lord. Why me? He would tell me how He chose me before I was in my mother's womb. He walked me down memory lane many times and showed me all the times His hand was upon my life. As I laid on the floor of that retreat, the Lord entered into the blanket I was under. The Lord required a promise from me. He told me He was about to release my hearts prayers but that I must always ensure I will let nothing come between He and I. The cost was great but it was crucial for my life to always stay behind Him. I remember crying to the Lord from my soul. I knew I truly didn't have an option. He chose me. He told me to preach the Gospel immediately, Acts 9:20. I remember being terrified to go for my minister's license. They asked a question on the test that I knew I had to tell the truth. I had to tell them who God called me to be. I knew it at this point. I remember driving into the parking lot and hearing God say when the elders ask you, tell them what I said. I sat in the car for what felt like an hour. The test was written so why would I have to say it. I'll just write it on the paper, turn it in and slide on out. That was the plan. He pressed me so hard and said do not hold your tongue when it is time to speak. Well as you can imagine, the time came when I was asked to speak it. I have to declare to the world whether man accepts it or not that I am called to open the eyes of the unbeliever and to turn them from their darkness and from the power of satan unto God, Acts 26:18. This may sound strange but I don't believe anyone in their right mind would take such a mantle upon themselves. It is a weight that no man can carry without God's anointing on their life. I had a dream regarding a purple heart. It was a military purple heart that was given to me in the mist of three white vases. If you know anything about the Purple Heart it is given to someone who sustained an injury during an act of bravery or even death. This dream scared me greatly. The Lord explained it to me in great detail and His voice is the only one who could give me comfort. I don't know exactly how this road is going to look or even what it will entail. What I do know is that the Spirit of the Lord God is upon me because the Lord have anointed me to preach good tidings unto the meek; he hath sent me to bind up the brokenhearted, to proclaim liberty to the captives and the opening of the prison to them that are bound; to proclaim the acceptable year of the Lord, the day of vengeance of our God, to comfort all that mourn Isaiah 61:1-2. Be strong and courageous is the word of the Lord. It is time for us all to walk in the purpose and call on our lives for if we don't many will perish. It is and has always been God's desire that none should perish and that all would come to repentance. Who are we holding back from salvation due to fear, shame, guilt and the past? I have not chosen Him but He has chosen me. I am a keeper of the flames, I am a trailblazer (word of the Lord) 01/30/17. This is the last piece to my healing, my deliverance and my unleashing. I declare to the world I know who I am, I know who I was and I know who I will be. I am Strong, I am Bold, I am Beautiful and I am FREE.

Prayers:

Forgiveness

Lord help me to forgive myself for the decisions, events and things that occurred in my past. Help me to come face to face with what were facts but not my truth. I will rehearse the truth of God over my life. My truth is that I am an overcomer. I am more than a conqueror through Jesus Christ. The word of God says that if we don't forgive, our father will not forgive us of our sins. I include myself in the process of forgiveness. I declare today that I forgive myself in Jesus name, Amen.

Prayers for our Children

Lord I come to you as the one you have appointed to intercede for my child. You saw me fit to safeguard her/his life in my womb. I praise you for such an honor and count myself as worthy to be used by you. I pray that no residue of sin, iniquity or adverse effects of my past will impact my child, in Jesus name. I pray that as I have been cleansed and washed by the blood of Jesus my intercession will fill in the gap for my child. I speak his/her innocence is restored in Jesus name. I speak no weapon formed against him/her will prosper and that I will fight for her/him in the spirit. Lord make me sensitive to discern the presence of the enemy and provide me with holy boldness by your Spirit, to call it down in Jesus name. Solidify the love of God in our home and between each other. In Jesus name, Amen.

Please leave a review for this book on Amazon.com.

AllThingsKingdombyJermika.org

Visit our online business at

MyrtleTreeHC.com

Made in United States
North Haven, CT
01 February 2023

31935230R00046